Life Coaching

Questions And Activities For Your Professional Life Coaching And Career Consulting Business

Table Of Contents

Introduction

Chapter 1 - What Makes a Good Life Coach

Chapter 2 - Why Life Coaching

Chapter 3 - Finding Your Niche in Business, Money, Health and Spirituality

Chapter 4 - Your Business Startup and Marketing

Chapter 5 - Top Five Life Coaching Activities and Strategies Explained

Chapter 6 - Top 10 Questions and Feedback Explained

Conclusion

Introduction

Thank you for downloading the book "Life Coaching: Questions and Activities for Your Professional Life Coaching and Career Consulting Business."

This book contains **essential lessons** on how you can pursue life coaching as a **powerful** career. Specifically, this book will **guide** you and help you understand the following topics:

- The right **mindset** and the characters and traits that make an **influential** life coach

- The different benefits for the person who receives life coaching such as **positive thinking**, **motivation**, **productivity**, and **performance**.

- The different life coaching niche you can choose from such as **career coaching**, **business coaching**, **leadership training**, **personal development**, and more.

- How to start your own life **coaching business** and **consulting** firm
- Top life coaching **activities** and **strategies** explained
- Top **questions** and feedback you can use during initial client conversation
- Consider this book as your beginner's manual in starting your wonderful yet overwhelming journey as a life coach.

Thank you again and I hope you enjoy this book!

Chapter 1 - What Makes A Good Life Coach

Many of us are excited about setting our life goals, especially at the beginning of the year, only to be disappointed because we have failed to achieve them because we have stopped working on them at the middle of the year.

There's no way we can predict the challenges that we will face in our lives, and usually our priorities will change as we go on. However, these things should not keep you from pursuing happiness and fulfilment in your life. A life coach can help someone to get back on track and continue working on achieving his life goals.

What is Life Coaching?

First things first, let's define life coaching.

Life coaching is a future-centric approach used to help people improve their lives. This is usually done through the establishment and achievement of personal as well as professional goals.

Even though this career may resemble the functions of a psychiatrist or a psychologist, life coaching is different. Life coaches don't look back on the past of their clients, and they merely evaluate areas in which the client may improve and provide advice on how they can improve.

Life coaches use different concepts to help their clients, some of which may include modifying their behavior, setting their goals, and mentoring. Coaching often takes place once or several times in a week, while life-coaching sessions could be done through personal meet-ups, email, or via phone.

The coaching process begins with an initial discussion in which the coach and the client agree to identify problems and together they find ways on how they can find solution to these problems.

The primary purpose of life coaching is to find inspiration or motivation from a coach who can encourage a person and push him to maximize your potential by making him more aware of the weaknesses and supporting him to overcome them.

What Makes a Good Life Coach?

Most importantly, a life coach cannot professionally guide you through a sticky situation or a rough time if they have never experienced struggles themselves. A life coach can be considered good, if he or she has a positive outlook in life, and practically applies it.

If you want to be a life coach, but you freak out when you think that someone has grabbed your parking spot, but advises her clients that divorce can be a helpful step to personally grow, you are not being genuine. Faking positive outlook will not really help your client.

Another important factor that life coach should take care is how he is organizing his own life. If you say to your client that you will call, but you fail to do so, then it is a red flag that he is not totally in control of his own life, and should probably not be entrusted with your life.

Finally, all life coaches should be properly licensed. Your advice to your client could make or break his life. Hence, it is crucial for a life coach to be knowledgeable and well-trained in this promising career.

Five Qualities of a Great Life Coach

There is a high chance that you grabbed this book because you are still trying to know if life coaching can be a great career for you. Many professional life coaches are blessed with a special way of seeing the perspectives of other people and they have the ability to help these people to act and clarify their actions.

There are universal traits that are very common among good life coaches. These traits are: authenticity, experience, insight, empathy, and great listener.

Authenticity

It is crucial that the life coach is authentic and transparent. In fact, this is the foundation life coaching, as without this trait, it can be difficult to build trust. Life coaches should not pretend what they are not. Never pretend that you have experienced specific problems if you have not. That will be an outright life. It is okay to be an amateur in this field. Many great life coaches begun their career as amateurs. By being yourself, you can help someone else to be more of who they are. Ultimately, this is the essence of life coaching.

Experience

It will be helpful if a life coach has already experienced how to cope, solve, or manage different problems in life. Experience can be a real bonus, depending on what you are coaching. A background in psychology can help you but it is not a requirement. Being worldly and real-life lessons from your experience could help you in dealing with your clients.

Insight

Insight refers to the ability of a life coach to discern the real nature of a situation. It is also the ability to see patterns. Most people who seek help from a life coach are living a complicated life or struggling with difficult situations at their work or at their relationships. Strong insight into what the person is dealing with is crucial to become an effective coach.

Empathy

Empathy is the character of someone to share his or experience without the need to go through the same experience. A life coach who is not empathetic may find it difficult to connect or communicate quite well with people. As a life coach, it is an important asset to be able to emphatize with your client even if you fail to personally experience what you are going through.

Great Listener

Listening is a core skill in life coaching. Most life coaches have a lot of things to share, and there is surely a component of teaching in this career. However, if you are not willing to relax and listen to what your client is telling, you may find it difficult to become an effective life coach.

Life coaching is an amazing career, surprisingly rewarding, and could be really profitable. If you have what it takes to become a life coach, be sure to read the following chapters to help you in your journey to this wonderful career.

Chapter 2 - Why Life Coaching

In starting your career as a life coach, you should ask yourself, "Is this the career that I am happy to spend my whole life with?". Turns out, many life coach answered yes to that question. However, unlike other careers, many life coach choose this profession because they can help people in changing their lives.

Benefits for the Person who Receives the Coaching

When you choose to become a professional life coach you can help many people to take control of their lives and head into the direction that will give them happiness and fulfilment.

Pursue Fulfilment in Life

Life is all about self-fulfillment. In whatever we do, we should always try to max out our fulfilment. As a life coach, you can help hundreds, even thousands of people to fulfil their life's potentials. A fulfilling life is a great outcome of great life coaching. As you help more people to fulfil their dreams, you will also share the same feeling of being fully alive. You will also fully appreciate and enjoy every moment and live in alignment with your life values and purpose.

Achieve Clarity

This is often the most difficult part to achieve. In this great diversity of choices, we have to choose, or life will choose for us. And through our years, we usually have to redefine our choices as we try to grow. What is important for your client three years ago is probably not what is really most important for him today. As a life coach, you can help your client to find clarity on his goals and on his life's purpose.

Strengthen Personal Foundation

Most people who seek help from a life coach wants more, and sometimes much more, and they are aware that they should make specific changes in their professional and personal lives to get more of what they really desire. These changes could take time and effort. As a life coach, you can focus on boosting the personal foundation of your client, as an approach to work on his life goals.

Improve Focus

As a life coach, you can help your clients create the plans that could maximize their desired results, without draining their life. Helping your client to focus on an effective plan of action is only 50% of the task ahead. Moving regularly towards the desired target is an important key. Even if your client is clear on what he wants, there is always the tendency for the mind to forget. Not because their goals are no longer essential, but because they could easily get caught up in life, get busy, and could be easily swayed. Your role as a life coach is to help your client to focus and keep the vision alive.

Find Balance

Every area of our life is linked to each other. If one area is out of sync, it will affect the other areas. If your client's life is out of balance, he or she is putting his energy in only one to two areas of his life, which could lead to energy depletion. As a life coach, you need to look at your client's life as a whole - from personal relationships, health, spirituality, finances, self growth, and more. As you try to focus on balancing every area of your client's life, you will also achieve peace of mind, more energy, and a deeper sense of self-fulfilment.

Foster Accountability

A commitment that you made only to yourself will easily be broken. But once you make a commitment to another person, especially if that person is not in your personal circle (a life coach), you will have the accountability to fulfil that commitment. Getting a life coach to verbally commit in a regular schedule will put more leverage on you so you can help your clients to fulfil their commitments.

Encourage Growth

Every human being has the need to learn and grow. As a matter of fact, people who have stopped growing and learning in life are considered walking dead. Personal growth and learning are among the most fulfilling and most satisfying experiences. As a life coach, you can encourage growth through life-long learning. You can entice clients who also love to learn and grow. Of all the reasons people seek the services of a life coach, the bottom line is change, which is equal for growth.

Find Life Purpose

Finding your life's purpose is a crucial element to seek a fulfilled life. People who are clear of their purpose in life and are really living their purpose each day, are usually fulfilled people. As a life coach, you can help your clients to identify their vision. The next step is to integrate this vision into their life.

Inner Wisdom

As a life coach, you have the opportunity to share your inner wisdom. Using the art of asking questions, and by listening to your clients, you can gain more wisdom as you work through this career.

Getting an Edge in Your Life and Career

Most people think that they can do everything they think about, and so they don't really need a life coach. To be honest, no one really needs a life coach. However, everyone could significantly benefit from a life coach. Guidance from a life coach will provide your client an edge over their colleagues who are not guided by a life coach. Having a life coach means having an edge.

Chapter 3 - Finding Your Niche in Business, Money, Health and Spirituality

There are many areas of life coaching, and each one can be profitable. While you can be a generalist life coach, finding your niche will give you the chance to focus more on one area for your specialization, so in the long run you will gain mastery of this niche.

How to Find Your Coaching Niche

The following are the factors that you need to consider in finding your life coaching niche:

> **Your Personal and Professional Background**
>
> For example, if your personal background is about parenting, or you have rich experience in managing a sales team, this can be a great factor in your choice of life coaching specialization.
>
> One life coach choose financial advice for seniors because he experienced how challenging it is to sort out the finances of his parents who had to retire without enough financial plan.
>
> You must consider what can share to your client on top of your professional training as a life coach.

Professional Qualifications

It will be helpful if you have other professional experience of qualifications. For example, if you are a licensed financial planner, fitness trainer, author, or real estate broker, that can also provide you an edge in when you like to find niche markets and improve your marketing strategies for a specific niche.

Niche Profitability

Probably you have the passion to work with a specific type of clients, but the market segment may not have the capacity to pay your coaching fee. For business sake, it is ideal to find a related demographics who can easily pay your fees. Once you are earning enough, it will be easy for you to take pro bono clients just for the sake of helping out people who are in need of your coaching service.

Life Coaching Niche

A life coach may have only one or several niche under their specialization, but they are also skilled at general life coaching strategies. Life coaching could help you work on specific areas, which could bring more success, happiness, and balance into your life.

You may work to enhance specific areas of your life like interpersonal skills, work-life harmony, setting personal and professional goals, time management, self-esteem, and stress management. Below are the common life coaching niche that you may choose to explore:

Health, Fitness & Wellness Coaching

A health, fitness, or wellness coach will help you focus on improving specific areas of your health and wellbeing. In this niche, you can help clients to help create strategies for getting in shape or losing weight, find ways to manage time properly to give room for health and fitness, effectively manage illness, and ways to increase vitality and reduce stress.

Parenting & Family Coaching

A parenting coach will help you to develop your own resources for the rewarding yet challenging job of being a mother or a father. Parenting could be extremely difficult without a string support network, and a parenting coach could help fill that gap.

A family coach helps people and their families to live a happy and healthy life. You may work on enhancing communication within the family, managing conflict or fortifying family bonds.

It can be lonely being a parent if you don't have a good support network, which is why having a coach on your side. A coach will cheer you on when you succeed and give you advice when you run into difficulties.

Relationship & Dating Coaching

A relationship coach generally helps clients to establish more successful relationships in their life. Clients can work individually with a relationship coach or with their partner. A relationship coach can help in improving communication, find more ways to cherish the relationship, and improve intimacy.

The associated field of dating coaching is targeted at helping clients to attract partners into their lives. A dating coach may work with their clients in overcoming their personal weaknesses such as shyness, or assist in finding the right partner in life.

Career Coaching

A career coach can help a person to find a job that he or she will love or one that will provide more satisfaction in his working life. A career coach can guide you in seeking promotion, achieving work-life balance, selecting the right career, and other relevant issues.

Creative Communication Coaching

A communication coach can help a person overcome any hindrances in his ability to share his or her thoughts with confidence and clarity. For example, if the client finds it fearsome to speak in a public place, a communication coach can help the client overcome this challenge. The relevant field of creativity coaching can help clients in tapping into their inner creativity, and overcome any hindrances.

Image Coaching

An image coach can help clients to create their winning strategies to create a positive public image. This is often needed by public personalities like politicians, celebrities, business leaders, and other important people.

Spiritual Coaching

Spiritual coaching could be focused on a particular faith like Christianity, or based more widely on finding harmony and balance with your spiritual nature.

Leadership Coaching

A leadership coach can help a person to excel in leadership roles by working on effective leadership strategies and changing areas that are non-productive. The relevant field of performance coaching can help a person to reach their performance goals and excel at their ventures.

Retirement Coaching

A retirement coach can work with people who are about to retire or already retired from their jobs. Prior to retirement, it is ideal to get advice on whether the retirement is the right option for you, and establish a retirement plan. After retirement, a retirement coach can help a person to deal with this crucial milestone in life by assisting in dealing with the changes that comes with retirement such as living a new lifestyle, managing income, and finding more productive ways to spend retirement.

Business Coaching

Starting a business is a crucial point in a person's life. A business coach can help entrepreneurs to launch a successful business, enhance work processes, build effective teams, create more productive business processes, earn more money, and many more.

Regardless of the niche or speciality you choose, you should go for an area that will really interest you and the type of clients that you enjoy working with. You need to figure out the special skills, experience, and knowledge that you can bring to coaching that you already have a passion.

Chapter 4 - Your Business Start Up And Marketing

Like many forms of business, the process of setting up your life coaching business could be overwhelming. Hence in this chapter, you will learn essential steps in setting up life coaching as your business. Going through these steps will save you time and money.

Step 1 - Find Your Life Coaching Niche

We have discussed a lot about finding your life coaching niche in the previous chapter. It is ideal to find a specialized niche in this business, as marketing general coaching services could be a challenge.

Remember, you are selling a service that is intangible and a product that is yet to be felt by your client. Thus, you need to emphasize the visible aspects of the current situation of your client, which in this kind of business, is the problem they have that you should help in fixing as a coach. Also known as the top-of-the-mind issue, this is the problem that usually haunts a client to the extent that they feel the need to pay so they can find plausible solutions.

The knowledge, skills, and tools that you can learn as a life coach could be applied to any context - relationships, health, career, business - as we have already covered in the previous chapter. In order to find clients and secure them permanently in your client's list, you need to specialize in solving particular problems.

It is perfectly fine if you find this quite confining. When you are already up and running, you could always expand your services and your customer base. It is okay to begin small and narrow, as variety will always be there for you. It is first important to be specific in your marketing by concentrating on setting up yourself as the top life coach when it comes to a specific set of problems.

Finding your niche is the primary step towards setting up a profitable and rewarding life coaching business. Once you complete this step, the rest of the steps will neatly fall into place.

Step 2- Give Your Life Coaching Business A Name

Giving your business a name could be exciting yet daunting task. A fast search online could lead you to believe that all good names are already in use. But this is far from reality. No matter how smart-sounding names appear to be, nothing could capture you as a professional life coach or the unique selling point of your service.

Take note that ultimately, people are seeking you because they trust you as a life coach. Hence, it is fine to use your name or a particular nickname for your life coaching business. This will not only associate a strong visual branding with your services, it will also help you establish your own unique brand.

Using your name for your life coaching business will allow you to improve top-of-mind awareness, which will keep you center and front with present and future customers. It will also allow you the freedom to offer more programs, products, and even change the kind of coaching you offer without the need to re-think of a totally brand new identity.

Another benefit of using your own name is that it could simplify buying the URL for your website. You should not be discouraged if your name is not yet available. You can try some alternatives. For instance, Will Brown may not be available, but Will.s.Brown or WillBrownCoaching could still be taken. Then, if you begin your own coaching firm, you can name it "Will Brown & Associates."

If you prefer to have a business name, which does not use any form of your name, you can create one that will speak to the solution that you are offering. As an example, one life coach has chosen the name "Calm Solution" to show her calm resolution and marriage coaching for those who are considering divorce. The concept here is that the name of the business should speak to your target client and the solutions that they are searching.

Step 3 - Choose the Suitable Structure for Your Life Coaching Business

There are six basic unique business structures in the US. They are the following:

- S Corporation
- Partnership
- Corporation
- Cooperative
- Limited Liability Company (LLC)
- Sole Proprietorship

Each structure provides different legal protections and comes with different tax obligations and benefits. You should choose a business structure that is suitable according to your business preferences and needs. If you wish to be alone in managing the business, you can choose sole proprietorship, but if you have partners, of course Partnership is suitable one. As you expand your business, you may choose between a corporation or an LLC.

Step 4 - Choose How You Will Provide Your Life Coaching Services

Most life coaches prefer to work with their clients in person. After all, this profession is heavily based on establishing a relationship. However, the option of online connectivity offers a wider reach and more comfort, both for you and your clients. This leads us into another step in the decision process: should you work from an office or from home?

Home Office Coaching

The decision to set up a life coaching office is really dependent on your budget and preferences. Working in an office has its benefits. It will provide your services a professional look, especially if you are planning to offer workshops and coaching in groups.

If you are not in need of a full-time space, you may choose to rent it or sub-lease it to other coaches or professionals who need office, if this is allowed. This is one way that many life coaches were able to afford their office space, when they were just starting out. As their business expands, and they are now in need of the space, they will just scale back on the subleasing.

But of course, there are drawbacks that you should take note. A physical office needs separate utilities, high-speed online connection, and phone services. These services could quickly add up based on your office location.

Another option you can try is to rent office spaces by the hour. There are spaces that you can rent as you need them. For instance, you can rent a whole conference room when you need to hold a group session. This is another way to start your practice without incurring too much cost.

Life Coaching From Home

In comparison to having an office for your life coaching practice, working from home has its own set of benefits like the following:

- No need to commute
- Save time because you don't need to sit in traffic
- Take breaks whenever you like
- Work whenever or wherever you want
- Work while you are near with your family

One possible disadvantage to remember: If you choose to work at home, you have to find a way to separate your work from your personal life. Don't do work while you are taking care of your kids or your pets.

In setting up your home office, you should set aside a place that is intended only for work. This will allow you to easily avoid temptations and distractions, which will help you to focus on your clients.

If you are planning to coach your clients mainly online or via phone, a home office could be a better option for you.

One good setup is an office located inside the property, which is similar to a bungalow or a guest house. This is in a separate location from your main house, so it has a more professional appeal but also provides the comfort of proximity.

Another alternative that you can try is a separate entrance into a private space of your home. But once you begin packing in the clients, a separate location is more recommended.

Step 5 - Selecting the Right Equipment and Web Platform For Your Life Coaching Business

Once you have already chosen your working space, the final step is to furnish this with the coaching tools you need. Many coaches need a good headset and phone to talk with their clients. It is ideal to find a landline with a wireless headset. However, a cell phone and a good noise-cancelling headset can also do the job.

Before you buy the tools, you need to consider the location of your life coaching business. As an example, there are life coaches who can still deliver their services while they are on travel using only a cellphone and a laptop.

But you should make certain that you have a contingency plan so you cannot disappoint your clients once your main communication channel fails to work. Online connection and wireless signals are not always reliable.

One of the best platforms used by life coaching professionals is Skype. This is free, accessible anywhere, easy to use, and can be accessed through different devices including tablets and smartphones. The only requirement in using Skype for your life coaching business is a fast online connection.

You can also invest in other popular virtual meeting platforms that for a minimal fee, can provide you more reliable service. This includes Fuze, WebEx, and Google Hangouts.

If you want to perform group coaching, you need to invest in seminar service/online meeting platform such as GoToMeeting or WebEx. These online platforms provide enhanced features and more options for managing participants or facilitating groups.

How to Market Your Life Coaching Business

Setting up your life coaching business is just the beginning of your wonderful yet could be overwhelming journey. After opening your life coaching business, you need to find the clients so you can sustain your choice. This is not a difficult task if you know the steps to follow, and you are aggressive in marketing your business.

Personal Branding

Personal branding refers to the process of marketing yourself as a life coach, what you can offer, and who will benefit from what you are offering. To help you in this step, it is ideal to write a brand statement, which is a combination of a personal statement and mission statement. This statement will sum up your brand and then create the resources to share this brand. You can develop a website, print brochures, and business cards.

Branding yourself doesn't need to cost a fortune. There are numerous sites online that you can turn into to set up your website for free or for a minimal cost. You can also find websites that allow you to design your own business cards and brochure and just print them out from your home.

Leverage On Your Experience

It is crucial to understand that building your new life coaching business takes time. Eventually, most of your clients will come to you based on personal referrals. You can use your personal and professional experience to your benefit. You can call former clients, co-workers, from previous jobs you have to let them know that you are now a life coach and offering your services.

Publish a Blog

Blogging is a rich source of finding new clients for your life coaching business. This platform will allow you to discuss about what you are doing every day. You can choose to post advice, life stories, helpful information, and anecdotes. Regardless of what you choose to blog, ensure that you are writing regularly and you can immediately respond to your potential clients.

Write Great Articles

It is ideal to write articles that are relevant to your niche, and post them to your blog. This is a good way for your potential customers to find your website and learn more about your life coaching business. Make sure that your writing shows who you are and will give a great indication of what you can offer. Through this, potential clients will read about your insights, and if they find it useful, they can forward it or share it through their social networking sites. Hence, you should ensure that your company name and contact details are included.

Tap Local Resources

Almost every town or city has a local networking club that meets regularly. This is often a forum where you can share details about yourself and your business, distribute flyers, and meet more people.

Prepare for the meeting ahead. Print your business cards and brochures, and be sure that your website is already up and running. Offer a free session to those who wish to know more about life coaching and offer discounts or freebies to those who can provide you with referrals.

Use Social Media Platforms

If you have an online business and you are working from home, you can use the power of the Internet. There are numerous websites today that are specifically focused on social and professional networking. Hence, make certain that you are present in top social networking sites such as Facebook, Twitter, Pinterest, LinkedIn, Instagram and other sites that are catering to your target market.

Be creative, flexible, and open when it comes to marketing your life coaching business. If one marketing strategy is not working well, sit for a while and think what is going wrong. Remember, you need people who are actually willing to pay for your services, and you can only reach them out through effective marketing.

Chapter 5 - Top Five Life Coaching Activities And Strategies Explained

In order to be an effective life coach, you need to follow a proven strategy. This will provide you a solid structure on how you can work with your clients and make sure that they will greatly benefit from your services. In this Chapter, we will discuss the top five coaching activities that you can follow as you start your career as a life coach:

Five Steps in Life Coaching Strategy

1. Clarify the Goal
2. Make it Happen
3. Plan for Action Strategy
4. Define Accountability
5. Celebrate Every Victory

Now, let us take a closer look at every step.

Step 1 - Clarify the Goal

The first step in your life coaching strategy is to define the goal of your client in one measurable and objective approach. To determine if your client has achieve his or her goal, regardless of its immensity, you and your client should exactly know what result they like and you should be able to keep track of the progress in a quantitative manner. Once your client is clear, you are also clear, and you both agree on the goals, they will begin to take on a new form of reality.

Step 2 - Make It Happen

Did you know that our subconscious mind doesn't know the difference between imagination and reality? The brain's chemical reaction are the same whether an experience is really happening or we are just imagining it. Hence, the more we imagine a scenario using our five sense, the higher the effect it could have.

In this step, allow your client to imagine vividly what it will be like once he achieves his goals. Ask your client where will they be, what they are doing and who are they with.

Make certain to have them imagine the experience using these senses - the scent they will smell, the things they will see, the sounds they will hear. In coaching your client in making the experience a reality in their mind, it will provide them a strong incentive to make the necessary steps to work on their goals.

Step 3 - Plan for Action Strategy

After establishing a well-defined and measurable goal, the next thing to do in the coaching process is to work with your client in order to come up with a strategic plan in achieving goals. Figure out the initial steps that your client should do as well as the timeframe to complete the goal.

The coaching strategy could be to begin at the end and work from the end goal to determine the best actions for your client to take. It is quite impossible that the goals of your clients will just fall from the sky. They need to implement focused action in order to reach their goals.

Step 4 - Define Accountability

It is crucial for you as a life coach to hold your client accountable for every step along the way. Monitor their commitments and ensure that they stick to them. Enforcing accountability for their actions will allow your client to feel that they are into real progress. This could lead to your client gaining significant confidence with their capacity to reach their goal with every action step that they successfully complete.

Step 5 - Celebrate Every Victory

It is ideal to acknowledge every step that your client takes on to work on his goal. This is an important part of the life coaching strategy. Some steps of the coaching strategy are easier compared to other, but they are all crucial in making seemingly impossible goals to be achieved by your client. In this step, it is crucial for your client to understand that celebrating every small victory is important and can encourage motivation to work further.

Using this simple life coaching strategy, large goals can be achieved within your time frame. You can use this strategy with your coaching clients and you can watch how fast they can realize their goals.

Chapter 6 - Top 10 Questions And Feedback Explained

If you like to attract more clients to enrol in your life coaching session, it is best to engage them in their own story and vision. Guide them to make them feel that there is a current gap in their life. Then tell them how you could help them as a life coach to fill that gap. Below are the top 10 questions and feedback that you can use to engage with your clients.

1. Establish a Connection

It is essential to first establish a connection and frame the conversation for success. Say something like this: "I am really excited to talk with you today. Is it okay if I ask you some meaningful and interesting questions about your _____ (health, marriage, business, or life)?"

2. Get a Fast Glimpse of Where The Client Is

This is important to assess the current status of your client. Say something like this: "Can you tell me a bit about what you feel today?"

3. Discover What They Really Like

Help your client uncover the things that he or she really likes. Say something like this: "If you can have everything you like in your _____ in the next three months, what will you feel?"

4. Assist Them to Connect Their Emotions With Their Vision

Emotional connection is important to forge a strong vision for your client. Say something like this: "Why does it matter if you achieve this goal?"

5. Ask About Your Client's Perceived Obstacles

You can ask your client to list their perceived obstacles and challenges that stops them from achieving their goals. Ask "What is stopping you from achieving this goal?" Just allow them to talk freely, and don't coach them.

6. Assist Them in Understanding the Value of Living with the Status Quo

This question is crucial to understand the cost of living with the norm. Ask something like "What was the effect of you not complying with _____?"

7. Help Them See the Bigger Picture

This will help your client to see a general perspective of his or her situation and appreciate the value of life coaching. Say something like this: "If you can overcome _____ (mention specific obstacle of the client) what would be the effect of that for you?

8. Identify the Takeaways

This is important step because it will allow your client to understand the gems that he gathered during the feedback session. Say something like this" What are the takeaways you got from our conversation?"

9. Invite them to Life Coaching

This is the time that you can share your life coaching system, explain the process, discuss the fees and terms, and explore the benefits of working with a life coach.

10. Enforce Urgency

Say something like this: Let's get started immediately. How about tomorrow?" Provide them a suitable first assignment that is easy yet powerful. Explain to them the next steps, and follow up right after by sending a welcome kit.

Conclusion

Thanks again for downloading this ebook!

I hope that this simple manual was able to help you learn and understand the basics of life coaching as a career that you can pursue.

Life coaching can be a rewarding career but with the required effort, you may find it a bit overwhelming especially during the initial setup days.

The next step is to apply the things you have learned here and continue working on your life coaching skills.

Thanks again and I hope you can also check out my other books!

Further Reading

If you liked the reading of this book and found helpful advice along the way, please also take the next step and have a look into other life-changing books by the author Thomas Keane.

Conversation Skills:

Tactics to Improve Your Conversation and Small Talk Skills for Better Social, Business and Relationship Communication

In this book, we will discuss the importance of having an effective conversation and communication skill and how to use it to your advantage. Many people lack this very important skill, but the good news is, conversation and communication skills can be acquired through learning and constant practice.
We will explore different strategies and techniques to improve your conversations at work and in relationships. We will also discuss ways to improve your presentation skills, so that you will never catch yourself lost for words ever again. Plus, we will also give you tips and tricks on how to approach someone and strike up a healthy and fun conversation.

ASIN: B01LBNE2BC

Challenge Yourself:

How to Be Happier and Live an Exciting and Fulfilling Life

Are you living a mediocre life? Are you merely floating through life without having a clear direction of where you are headed? Are you not living the kind of life that you want and deserve? If you answered yes to any of the questions, then it is time for a change. It is time to take the challenge and live a better and more fulfilling life. It is not too late to reclaim your power to transform your life and live a better and happier life. In this book, you will learn proven tips and techniques that will help you push yourself to live a better and fulfilling life. In this book, you will learn various tips and techniques that will help you live a more fulfilling, meaningful, and fun life.

ASIN: B00X2UX7IW

Smartphone Addiction:

How to Overcome Smartphone Addiction and Reconnect to Real Life

Discover the cause of smartphone addiction and overcome it so you and friends and family can start to more deeply reconnect to each other again and have a whole new life experience.

Smartphones have become an indispensable part of our lives. They bring a lot of advantages with them, yet they have some downsides. Some years ago, no one would have thought that smartphones could once control the lives of so many people and that a thing called smartphone addiction would be an actual condition. This book explores this unique and modern condition and provides a detailed account of what it is, what its symptoms and triggers are and most importantly, how you can reclaim control over it and prevent it from wreaking havoc on your life.

ASIN: B00TKD7S30

Positive Parenting
Parenting Guide And Methods For A Positive Child Development

Positive Parenting will help you discover the keys to raising a social, confident, optimistic, creative, healthy and happy child.

Follow the specific guide and methods described to ensure a positive child development. If you put this advice into practice you will find yourself enjoying a close relationship with your child. Your Child on the other hand will grow up well-behaved and build physical and mental strength for the life ahead.

You are responsible for your child's development and helping them build a strong emotional foundation of self-respect, resourcefulness and creativity. If you teach your child while they are still young, they will be able to acquire those traits and turn them into habits. **ASIN:**

ASIN: B01EYF3YX6

Copyright 2016 - All rights reserved.

This document is geared towards providing exact and reliable information in regards to the topic and issue covered. The publication is sold with the idea that the publisher is not required to render accounting, officially permitted, or otherwise, qualified services. If advice is necessary, legal or professional, a practiced individual in the profession should be ordered.

- From a Declaration of Principles which was accepted and approved equally by a Committee of the American Bar Association and a Committee of Publishers and Associations.

In no way is it legal to reproduce, duplicate, or transmit any part of this document in either electronic means or in printed format. Recording of this publication is strictly prohibited and any storage of this document is not allowed unless with written permission from the publisher. All rights reserved.

The information provided herein is stated to be truthful and consistent, in that any liability, in terms of inattention or otherwise, by any usage or abuse of any policies, processes, or directions contained within is the solitary and utter responsibility of the recipient reader. Under no circumstances will any legal responsibility or blame be held against the publisher for any reparation, damages, or monetary loss due to the information herein, either directly or indirectly.

Respective authors own all copyrights not held by the publisher.

The information herein is offered for informational purposes solely, and is universal as so. The presentation of the information is without contract or any type of guarantee assurance.

The trademarks that are used are without any consent, and the publication of the trademark is without permission or backing by the trademark owner. All trademarks and brands within this book are for clarifying purposes only and are the owned by the owners themselves, not affiliated with this document.

Made in the USA
Lexington, KY
13 May 2017